Introduction

This book introduces another unique cutter - The Lacy Heart - which can be used to make all kinds of decorations including fantasy flowers, borders, cradles, umbrella etc. It gives a few more ideas for the Unbreakable Gel (UG) and covers the making of Gelatine flowers and leaves. It also shows delightfully delicate textured rolling pins - the Angel Hair pins - available in two sizes 10" and 7". See rear cover.

Variations on the 'Varipin' are included - a mini-pin and a tapered textured tool. In a new departure I have incorporated some enchanting lace cutters designed by Diana Cattel from Devon Ladye

The Tools. General Notes:

Non-stick.	One of the most useful aspects of their design is their non-stick property which is inherent in the material used. It is not a surface finish and, therefore, cannot wear off.
Materials.	All the tools can be used with any soft material such as flowerpaste, sugarpaste, marzipan, modelling chocolate, plasticine, modelling clay, cold porcelain, etc.*
Temperature.	They will withstand boiling water or the dishwasher without deforming.
Handles.	All the cutters have comfortably sized hollow handles which allow you to exert firm pressure over the whole of the cutting edges.
Stability.	They will not rust, corrode, deform or wear out with normal usage.
Marking.	All the tools are permanently marked to aid easy identification.
Metal.	They should not be brought into contact with sharp metal objects which may damage the cutting edges or surfaces. i.e. keep them separated from metal cutters.
Hygiene.	The materials meet the appropriate EEC Regulations for food hygiene.
Endorsement.	All the items are personally endorsed and used by PAT ASHBY, our Technical Director, who is one of the leading teachers of sugarcraft in the UK and is an International Judge, author and demonstrator.

*These cutters, as with all Orchard cutters, can be used very effectively with an air drying non-edible paste (Cold Pc

GW00367706

1

THE NEW TOOLS *(See Illustration 1)*.
(Full size cutout shapes are shown in Illustrations 1B & 1C).

The Lacy Heart Set (LH1, LH2, LH3, LH4).
This unique set of cutters can make delicate flower-like decorations, or side and corner pieces. They can be used to make ethereal looking collars or cradles. Because the effect is created by one press of the cutter, it is very easy for anyone to try out their skills. The results are only limited by your imagination. They are ideal for beginners since everything you do is right!

The Angel Hair Pins. There are two of these - a 10" and 7" mini-pin which produce a very delicate pattern when rolled over soft paste - see rear cover.

The Mini-Varipin and Varipin Tool. The mini-pin is a smaller 6" version of the popular 'Varipin' textured rolling pin.

The tool has two tapered textured ends ideal for giving that extra finish to your frilling. (See Illustration1A).

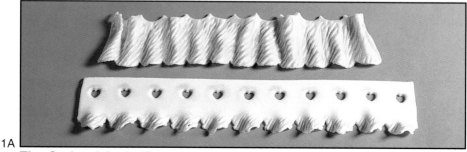

1A

The Orchard Arch. This 6¼" high perspex arch can form a simple but attractive cake top decoration when draped with flowers or bells. (See Illustrations 62-65).

The Lace Cutters. These delicate designs from Devon Ladye (Diana Cattel) make excellent side or top decorations. (See Pages 12 & 35).

LH1 (90mm)

LH2 (75mm)

1B

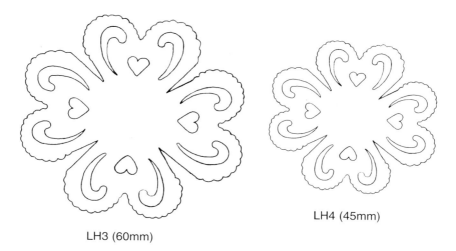

LH4 (45mm)

LH3 (60mm)

1C

How to make the Christmas Flower with the Lacy Hearts *(See Illustration 2).*

Smaller Flower. (Make 2).

1. Tape a cluster of White stamens onto a 24 gauge wire.

2. Roll out Green flowerpaste and cut out 2 Calyx cutters R11D and mark down the centre of each sepal. Glue the centre of one, place the other calyx on top, interleaving the sepals.

3. Dust Gold Green. (See Illustration 3).

4. Roll out Red flowerpaste and cut out one Lacy Heart LH3. Take out the inserts with the tip of the veining tool. Dust the centre Majestic Gold.

5. Glue the centre of the top calyx and place the Lacy Heart on top. Transfer the flower to the flowerstand (S1) over a large hole. Glue the base of the stamens and thread through the centre of the flower. Using 'Cloud Drift' (Acrylic fibre used to stuff toys), tuck in between the layers to shape the flower. (See Illustration 4). Leave to dry thoroughly. When dry, steam to set the colours.

Larger Flower. (Make 1).

Repeat steps 1-5 using Calyx cutter R11F and Lacy Heart cutter LH2.

6. For the UG twirls see Page 19.

2

3

4

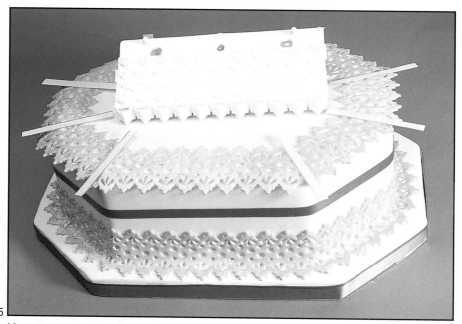

5

How to make the Lace Collar *(See Illustration 2).*

1. Coat the cake with Ivory sugarpaste and leave to firm. Insert a fan blade (LA2F) into hole 1 of the lace cutter body, 2 star blades (LA2E) into holes 2 and 3 and a second fan blade into hole 4. (See Illustration 5).

2. Measure the top of the cake for the length and width of the collar. Roll out lace paste (Recipe A) and cut out the required length with the assembled lace cutter. Move the cutter down to the appropriate width and cut again to give the same serrations on both edges. Leave the paste for ½ a minute or so and remove the inserts with the pointed end of the petal veining tool. Cut to shape - 8 pieces - and leave to dry on a dusted board.

3. When completely dry paint the sections of the collar with Majestic Gold and alcohol. Leave to dry.

4. The base decoration is made in a similar way, but while it is still soft, brush the underside with water and place into position round the cake. When dry, painting has to be done on the cake, so care is required to protect the board.

5. Paint the underside of the pieces from Step 3 with Tylose glue and place into position on the top.

6

How to make the Lacy Heart Cot with shade *(See Illustration 6).*

1. Roll out flowerpaste and cut out one Lacy Heart LH2. Remove inserts.
2. Dust the centre Bridal Satin and edges Orchid Mauve. Over dust with Cerise Sparkle.
3. Place in an apple tray to dry curved.
4. Roll out flowerpaste and cut out one Lacy Heart LH3. Remove inserts. Repeat steps 2 & 3 but prop shape with a little 'Cloud Drift' to obtain a tighter curve. (See Illustration 7).
5. Repeat steps 2 & 3 with Lacy Heart LH4.
6. Mash down flowerpaste with egg white or water to make a glue.
7. Hook the end of a 26 gauge White wire. Turn the hook at right angle and curve the wire into a semicircle. Glue the hooked end to the inside centre of the LH4. Leave to dry thoroughly.

To assemble the cot:

8. Turn over LH2 for the base and glue the centre. Place the upturned LH3 on top. Slide the base of the curved wire between LH2 and LH3. Prop and leave to dry thoroughly
9. Roll out flowerpaste and cut out Blossoms. One each of F2, F2M and F2S.
10. Dust the edges Alpine Rose. Put a little Rose water in the centre of F2, place F2M on top, interleaving and the same for F2S. Pop on sponge and press in the middle with the balling tool (OP1) to cup.
11. When dry glue to the top of the 'shade'. When dry, pop a baby in the centre of the cot. Steam to set the colour.

Side Border *(See Illustration 8)*.

1. Cut out a strip of lace border (LB1) according to the circumference of the cake. Cut to the required width with the lace cutter (LA1) to give a serrated top edge. Using the heart blade (LA2B) cut out heart holes on the board as illustrated. (Make sure they are the right way up!). Leave to set a minute and then remove the hearts with the pointed end of the petal veining tool (OP2).

2. Paint the underside with Tylose glue and fit round the cake. Trim as necessary.

3. Cut out several lacy hearts and dust them as required. Glue them into position round the base of the cake with water or Royal Icing.

9

Embossing *(See Illustrations 9 & 10).*

1. While the cake covering is still soft, press a lacy heart cutter into the side at regular intervals round the cake, previously measured.

10

11

Side Cutouts *(See Illustration 11).*

1. Use the unwanted hearts and florets from a lacy heart cutter as decorations on the side of a cake. Stick with Rose water.

12

How to make the Lacy Heart Ring Case Cake *(See Illustration 12).*
Ring Case:
1. Roll out White flowerpaste and cut out two Lacy Hearts LH3. Remove the inserts. Dust the outside Majestic Gold, the inside tips Leaf Green and the centre Bridal Satin. Set one LH3 in an apple tray and curve the other just inside the base, and overhanging to form the lid, propping it with 'Cloud Drift'. Leave to dry thoroughly.

2. When dry press a ball of sugarpaste into the base and press the ring into the soft paste. (Remove the ring once the sugarpaste is dry).

3. Dust with Bridal Satin. When dry, cut out several heart shapes using the heart blade (LA2A) from the Lace Cutter (see Book 8). Dust with Majestic Gold. Glue to the edge of the circle on the base and create a circle of hearts on the 'lid' of the ring case. The stand is one Lacy Heart LH1. Dust as above. (See Illustration 13).

Collar:
4.Roll out White flowerpaste and cut out eleven Lacy Hearts LH4. Remove the inserts. Dust the centres with Bridal Satin, the outside Majestic Gold and the tips Leaf Green.

5. Cut out several heart shapes using heart blade LA2A from the Lace Cutter (See Book 8). Dust Leaf Green and glue to the centre of the Lacy Heart shape. (See Illustration 12).

6. Leave to dry thoroughly. Mash down some White flowerpaste with egg white or water and glue the Lacy Hearts around the cake.

13   14

Base Border:

7. Roll out White sugarpaste and cut out seven Lacy Heart shapes LH3. Leave the inserts in and dust the same as the collar shapes. While still soft glue to the base of the cake. (See Illustration 14).

8. Roll out White sugarpaste and cut out two Lacy Hearts LH3. Cut into 4 sections. Leave the inserts in. Dust the whole Bridal Satin and the heart Majestic Gold. Steam all the Lacy Hearts to set the colour. Glue to the board in between the LH3's.

15

How to make the Lacy Bell Cake *(See Illustration 15)*.
Lacy Bell Flower:
1. Tape with Light Green tape one long Gold stamen and 5 shorter stamens onto a 24 gauge wire. Dust the stems of the stamens Super Green.
2. Roll out flowerpaste and cut out one Lacy Heart LH4. Remove the inserts. Dust the base Majestic Gold and the tips Orchid Mauve. Over dust the Mauve with Cerise Sparkle.
3. Make a hole in the centre using the taped stamens - remove and leave the Lacy Heart to set in a cupped position, colour on the outside.
4. Roll out flowerpaste and cut out one 6 petal cutter N5 and one 6 petal cutter N6. Dust with Bridal Satin, the centre Super Green Sparkle, and the tips of the petals Orchid Mauve. Over dust the Mauve with Cerise Sparkle. Pinch the tips of the petals.
5. Glue the centre of N5 and place N6 on top, alternating the petals.
6. Glue the base of the stamens and thread through the centre of N5 and N6, turnover and glue the centre to create a bell shape with LH4 from Step 3 and thread up the wire to fit snugly under the petals. (See Illustration 16).
7. Leave to dry thoroughly. When dry, steam to set the colours. The Devon Ladye Bobbin & Regent Lace cutters are used as a border. (See Illustration 17).

16

17

18

How to make the Umbrella Cake with Gelatine Primulas
(See Illustration 18).

Basic instructions. See Gelatine Recipe (Page 46).

Stamens
Use any stamens which will compliment your flower. I have used Pearl stamens for the Pale Pink spray. You can also dip your stamens into the gelatine mixture if you wish to match the texture of your flower.

Petal Shape:
1. Decide which flower or leaf you wish to copy and find the appropriate width of rolling pin or dowel for the wire to be wrapped around. I found the Orchard 1/2" rolling pin a good size.

2. You require 28 or 30 gauge White wire cut into 3. The smaller the leaf or petal the thinner gauge wire you require.

3. Should you require coloured wires then put colour in the centre of a small piece of sponge. Place the wire in the centre, squeeze the sponge either side and pull the wire through the colour. Leave to dry.

4. Make all your shaped wires for each arrangement before you start dipping. (See Illustration 19).

5. Wind the wire around the rolling pin and twist tightly at the base to form a circle. Remove the wire from the pin.

6. To form a heart shape, hold the circle either side and use the handle of a paint brush or cocktail stick to press in the centre of the circle to form the heart shape. Hold the heart in your fingers and bend the wire down so it can be dipped horizontally into the liquid. Should you require a 'natural' look then bend your petal slightly over the pin.

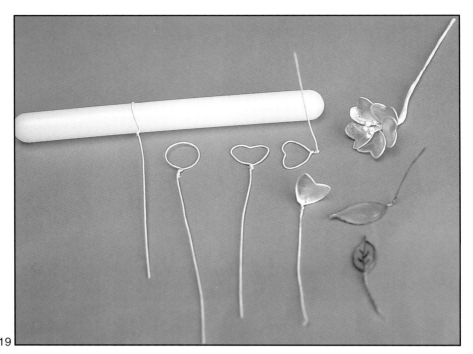

7. Dip one shape at a time. Remove the surplus on the side of the cup. Hold for a couple of seconds and place in dry oasis to dry. Should it fail to adhere to the wire simply re-dip. The drying period will take at least an hour. The gelatine film should feel like paper.

To assemble the flower:

8. Fold three stamens in half, cut and tape to a 26 gauge Green wire.

9. Tape 5 petals around the stamens interleaving them. Tape in the one position so that they are all at the same height.

10. Repeat Steps 1-9, two more times making 3 flowers.

Leaves:

You will require 30 leaves.

Repeat Steps 1-5.

11. Pinch the top of the circle to make a simple leaf. Curve at this stage if required.

12. Bend the wire down at the base of the leaf and repeat Step 7 above (Petal).

13. To mark the veins in the leaves, take a fine paintbrush - mix your powder with a little alcohol. I use Vodka - wipe surplus off on kitchen roll and paint on the veins. Should you require any shading this is done in the same way. Let it dry.

14. Tape 3 leaves onto a 26 gauge wire - one at the top and one either side to form a triangle. Repeat this 10 times.

To Assemble the Spray *(See Illustration 20)*.

Tape the three flowers onto a 26 gauge wire forming a triangle. Tape one branch of leaves behind the top flower, and one branch either side, cutting off the surplus wire at an angle as you tape down the stem. Position the fourth branch facing the flowers, tape and bend the branch down to form a diamond shape.

Side of Cake

While the Sugarpaste coating is still soft, emboss around the sides using the medium primrose cutter F3M. When dry dust with Alpine Rose. Pipe 3 tiny White dots in the centre of each flower.

Base Board

Using a bradawl make a hole in the sugarpaste and through the board. Insert the branch into the board and push the dried sugarpaste around the wire to firm up. Repeat this 6 times.

Umbrella *(See Illustration 21)*.

1. Roll out flowerpaste and cut out one Lacy Heart LH1. Make a hole in the centre big enough for the handle to lodge in. Leave to dry in an apple tray. Roll a sausage tapered at the end, long enough to represent a handle for the umbrella. Curve at the end. The top of the umbrella is a cone. Leave to dry.

2. When dry dust the edges of the umbrella Alpine Rose and the rest Bridal Satin. 'Glue' the handle in the centre of the umbrella with sugarpaste mashed with water or egg white and the cone on top. When thoroughly dry, steam. Hook the bottom of the spray around the handle.

21

How to make the Mauve Lacy Flower Cake *(See Illustration 22)*.

1. Tape with Light Green tape one long Gold stamen and 5 shorter stamens onto a 24 gauge wire. Dust the stems of the stamens Super Green.

2. Roll out flowerpaste and cut out two Carnations C1M. Lengthen the long cuts with a palette knife. Frill each section with the petal veining tool. Dust with Bridal Satin, the centre with Super Green Sparkle and the tips of the petals Orchid Mauve. Over dust the Mauve with Cerise Sparkle. (See Illustration 23). Place in the flowerstand (S1) and cup with the balling tool.

3. Glue the base of the stamens from Step 1 and thread through the centre of both Carnations. Leave to dry.

4. Roll out flowerpaste and cut out one Lacy Heart LH1. Remove the inserts. Dust the base Majestic Gold and the tips Orchid Mauve. Over dust the Mauve with Cerise Sparkle.

5. Make a hole in the centre of an apple tray and Lacy Heart and leave to set in a cupped position.

6. Glue the base of the Carnations and thread through the Lacy Heart to fit snugly into the petal. Leave to dry thoroughly. When dry, steam to set the colours.

Leaves

7. Roll out White flowerpaste leaving a thick ridge at the base. Cut out 8 leaves with the Swan Tail cutter SW3. Push a glued 33 gauge wire into the thickened base. Soften the edges with the balling tool (OP1) on the pad (PD1) and mark a central vein with the petal veining tool. Dust the centre Leaf Green and over dust with Gold Green. Dust the remainder with Majestic Gold. When dry, steam.

8. Tape the leaf wires to the Lacy Heart stem and arrange the leaves symmetrically. (See Illustration 24).

9. The collar is made in the same way as for the Christmas Cake (See Page 4).

22

23

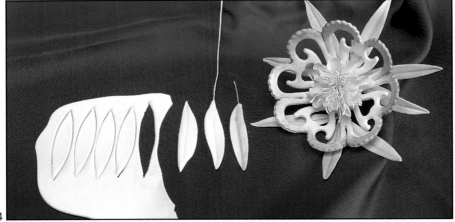

24

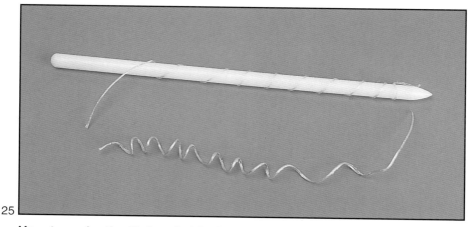

25

How to make the Unbreakable Gel Twirls *(See Illustration 25)*.

1. Make up one teaspoon of clear unbreakable gel according to the instructions on the packet.
2. Using a No.2 piping tube pipe straight lines onto a plastic sleeve. Leave overnight to dry.
3. Dampen one strand at a time. Leave approx. 1" straight and curl the remainder round a Slimpin. Allow to dry for approximately 15 mins.
4. When dry paint with Majestic Gold and alcohol.
5. Tape several twirls together. Cut to size and shape with scissors.

26

UG Celebration Cakes:
How to make the UG Filigree *(See Illustration 26)*.

1. Pipe the UG with a No.2 tube onto a plastic sleeve following Template 26T on Page 45, making sure the joins touch. Leave to dry (and shrink) overnight. Push the ends into a small ball of sugarpaste already positioned on the cake and trim as required with scissors. Conceal join with a flower.

27

How to make the UG Trellis *(See Illustration 27).*
1. Pipe the UG with a No.2 tube onto a plastic sleeve following Template 27T on Page 45, making sure the joins touch. Leave to dry (and shrink) overnight. Push the ends into a small ball of sugarpaste already positioned on the cake and trim as required with scissors. Conceal join with a bell. The bells are shown in Book 14.

28

How to make the Sunset Flower Cake *(See Illustration 28)*.

(This cake first appeared in Cake Craft Magazine).

1. Coat a 14" oval board with Egg Yellow sugarpaste, Mark the position of the 10" teardrop cake on the board. Indent the surface of the sugarpaste with the 'Varipin' in a fan shape by holding one end where the centre of the curve in the teardrop will be and rolling round the board, alternately roll and press firmly to give a wave effect. Leave to set.

2. Cover the cake with Egg Yellow sugarpaste. Leave to dry.

3. Wind 2 pieces of rose wire round a bunch of stamens about ½" from the tips, top and bottom. Cut in half. Place the tips together and wind a further piece of rose wire around the two bunches about ¼" from the top. Snip the original wires off. (See Illustration 29).

4. Trim the bottom of the bunch into a V shape. (The number of bunches required will depend on the size of the individual stamens). Thread a hooked 26 gauge wire through the bunch and tape down with Green florists tape. Paint some of the tips with Orchard Rose Leaf - to match the lace leaves.

5. Roll out Orange flowerpaste and cut out 1 Five-petal flower F6C. Fold 3 of the petals in, to make it easier to move onto the pad. This helps to make sure the petals do not stretch.

6. Flap over the petals on either side of the petal you wish to work on. This allows you to soften the edges of the inside of the petal easily. Vein the petal with the 'Varipin' tool and soften the edges with the balling tool (OP1). Repeat for the remaining petals.

7. Repeat Steps 5 and 6 with 1 F6B cutter.

8. Fold the petals in as for Step 5 and move onto a piece of kitchen roll for dusting. Dust the edges of the petals and also from the centre outwards with Alpine Rose - use a soft ⅜" brush. Repeat for F6B petal. (See Illustration 30).

9. Put glue in the centre of the F6C petal and place F6B on top, alternating the petals.

10. Move to the flowerstand (S1) and place the centre of the flower over a hole. Glue the base of the stamens from Step 4 and thread through the centre of the flower.

11. Prop and cup the petals to shape using the tip of the petal veining tool and 'Cloud Drift'. Leave to dry. (See Illustration 31). Repeat these steps using cutters F6B and F6 for a slightly smaller flower.

12. Once dry, steam the flower by twirling it for a few seconds in the steam of a boiling kettle. This blends in the colour. Leave to dry.

Bud *(See Illustration 32)*.

13. Make a cone from Orange flowerpaste. Mark curved vertical grooves round the bud with a fine palette knife. Dust the tips and grooves with Alpine Rose. Steam when dry.

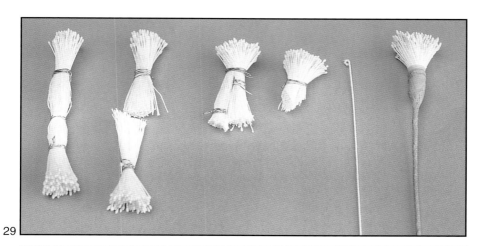

29

30

31

-21-

14. Roll out Rose Leaf coloured flowerpaste and cut out two Lace Leaves LL3. Remove the centres and leave to dry flat. Cut out a further three Lace Leaves LL4 to fit around the bud. Remove the centres and keep covered.

15. Glue the base of the bud and wrap the three LL4 leaves round the bud. Leave to dry.

Butterfly.

16. Roll out Light Orange flowerpaste and cut out one Butterfly B1. Fold up the wings and leave to dry. Paint the butterfly with a '000' paintbrush and Orchard Chocolate Brown mixed with water or alcohol. Make certain you paint the top and underneath. It is a good idea to copy from a butterfly book.

17. Stick the cake to the board with a little sugarpaste moistened with boiled water. Leave to dry.

18. Tear Orange florists tear-ribbon into ¼" and ½" wide strips. Moisten the ¼" ribbon with water and place round the base of the cake. Stick the ½" tape round the edge of the board with double-sided sticky tape. Mash down Yellow sugarpaste with a little boiled water and put it in an icing bag to attach the flowers, leaves and butterfly to the cake.

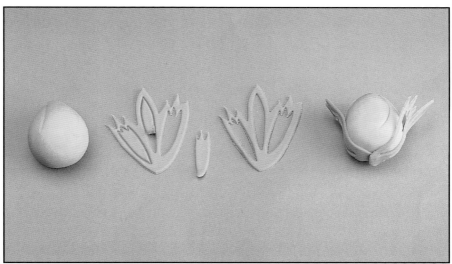

32

How to make the Snowman Cake *(See Illustration 33).*
(This cake first appeared in Cake Craft Magazine)
1. Coat the cake and board with sugarpaste. Roll the 'Varipin' around the board to obtain the frosty look. Dust the board with Hi-lite Blue and Hi-lite White. Leave to firm.
Border.
2. Roll out White flowerpaste. Roll again with the 'Varipin'. Cut out 21 Lace Leaf shapes with LL4. Remove the inserts. Dust with Hi-lite White and leave to dry. Steam.
Holly Leaves.
3. Roll out Holly Green concentrate flowerpaste and cut out 17 Holly shapes using Orchard Holly cutter H3.
TIP: Leave a thick piece of paste at the end to make for easier handling. Vein with the Rose Leaf veiner R10.
4. Remove to the Pad and 'bounce' the balling tool on each of the holly points. Twist to shape and leave to dry. When dry dust with Gold Green. Steam.
Holly Berries.
5. Make 24 berries using Red sugarpaste. Leave to dry. When dry paint with Confectioners' glaze.
TIP: Put the confectioners' glaze bottle in a small marmalade jar so it will not tip over.

33

The figures are wholly made from Lace Paste. (See Illustration 34).
Snowman.
6. Roll paste into a ball and then a slight cone for the body. Press in the top of the cone for the head to fit snugly on.
7. Roll paste into a ball for the head. Indent with the balling tool for the eyes. Using the veining tool press in for the nose hole. Cut a straw and use for a snowman smile.
TIP: You can cut any size of straw to make different sizes of smiles!
8. Leave to firm on a sponge.

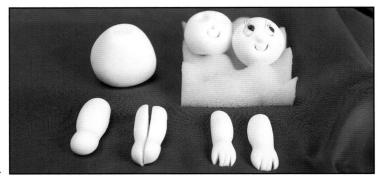

34

35

9. Roll paste into a sausage shape for the arms. Indent the top with the outside of your little finger. Cut in half lengthways. Flatten the ends. Cut out a triangle for the thumb and two cuts for the fingers.

10. Use a small ball of sugarpaste for the nose. Attach with Rose water and press in the hole.

11. Paint in the eyelashes with Brown and a '000' paintbrush.

12. To make the eyes mash down sugarpaste in White and Dark Brown and put in two separate piping bags without a tube. Using the piping bag with the White paste in, cut off enough to represent a No.2 piping tube. Push the end into the eye hole and pressure pipe for the white of the eyes. Leave to set.

13. With the Brown bag cut off enough to represent a No.1 piping tube, pressure pipe the pupil slightly off the edge of the white. Leave to dry.

Mrs Snowman *(See Illustration 35).*

Repeat Steps 5 to 13 only on a slightly smaller scale.

14. Roll out White flowerpaste and then roll again with the 'Varipin'. Cut out five Lace Leaf shapes with LL4. Remove the inserts. Attach with Rose water around her waist to form a skirt. Dust with Hi-lite Blue and Hi-lite White. When dry, steam.

15. Assemble the two figures close together and wrap the arms around each other to cuddle up.

36

Snowman's Hat *(See Illustration 36).*

16. Use a small ball of Brown sugarpaste. Pop into a plastic bag and gently stroke out around the centre to make the edges very thin. Leave a thicker piece in the centre. Remove from the plastic bag.

17. Roll out another small ball of Brown sugarpaste and place in the centre. Stroke gently around the edges so the hat becomes one.

18. Make an indentation in the centre with a knife. Using the piping bag with the Brown sugarpaste, stick the three sprigs of holly and berries on the side of the hat. Glaze the berries with Confectioners' glaze. Attach the hat to the head with the bag of soft White sugarpaste.

Ruff.

19. Roll out Red flowerpaste and cut out one six petal N2. Remove to pad and vein each petal down the centre with the pointed end of the veining tool. Glue to the top of the body and then glue the head onto the ruff.

Mrs Snowman's Hat.

20. Roll out Red flowerpaste and cut out one six petal N3, N4 and N5. Remove to pad and vein each petal down the centre. Starting with N3, glue one onto each other, interleaving. Glue a tiny cone in the centre of N5 to complete the hat. Glue the hat onto the head of Mrs Snowman and curve to shape.

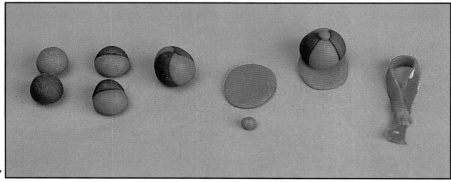

37

Snow Boys *(See Illustration 37).*
Repeat Steps 5 to 13 only on a slightly smaller scale.
Cap.
21. Shape equal balls of Red and Green sugarpaste. Cut each in half. Place Green next to Red. Then put one set on top of the other, alternating the colours. Roll together in the palm of your hand to create a ball.
22. Flatten a ball of Red paste to make the brim. Stick the ball from Step 21 at the back of the brim. Tiny Red ball goes on top of the cap to complete. Glue to the top of the head.
Scarf.
23. Roll a strip of Red sugarpaste and snip both ends with scissors. Wrap around the neck.
To Assemble.
24. Glue the figures into position and make snowballs and glue onto the cake. Glue a wide Green ribbon around the base of the board. A narrow Green ribbon around the base of the cake. Glue the lace leaves (points facing down) around the cake. Glue a narrow ribbon around the top of the lace leaves. Glue two holly leaves and three Red berries near the top of the cake and the top of the lace leaves leaving two lace leaf spaces in between.

38

How to make the Drapes of Autumn Gold
(See Illustration 38, also Book 14).

(This cake first appeared in Cake Craft Magazine).

Use Lace Paste (Recipe A). OR use equal amounts of flowerpaste and sugarpaste OR whatever you use to make your Garrett frills.

Coat oval cake in Ivory sugarpaste. Leave to firm.

1. Coat the board in the same colour and run the Orchard 'Varipin' over the surface around the board. Place the cake in the centre of the board and cut round the cake. Lift the cake out and remove the inner surplus sugarpaste. Place the cake in the centre. Allow to firm.

2. Using a paper till roll, measure and make a template to fit around the cake. Divide the template into equal sections (which will be the size of the drapes) measuring the length and depth of the drapes you require. (Suggestion: 6 for an 8" dia. cake). Mark the side of the cake with a scriber or with a piping tube.

3. Once you have the length and depth of the drape, cut out a paper template. (Suggestion: see Template 38T). Use the forming rod shape as the bottom curve. Top curve to choice. Angle the ends. The template for this cake should nearly reach to the base of the cake. I used 'mashed down' Ivory sugarpaste with a little water. Pop in a piping bag and pipe away. Very useful if you do not have any Royal Icing made up! Pipe a small bead or shell around the base border. Roll out Lace Paste, Roll the 'Varipin' over the paste.

4. Place template on top and cut out. A very thin palette or plastic knife is useful for this purpose as it does not damage the non-stick board.

5. Dust the underside of the paste with cornflour.

6. Place the rods on the board, shortest one at the top, and place the drape on top of the rods. Smooth in between with the balling tool. (Fingernails tend to mark the paste!).

7. Squeeze the ends of the rods together. You can dust the drapes at this stage if you wish.

8. Leave for about 30 seconds and then slide the rods out.

9. Put paste glue on the underside and in between the folds of the drapes. Glue underside of the top and base curves and place it in position on the side of the cake.

10. Cut off the top surplus. Continue around the cake. Leave to firm. Cover the board should you wish to dust the drapes on the cake. Colours I used for the drapes were Yellow, Majestic Gold, Orange and Perfect Red. Colour the board mostly Majestic Gold with a little Yellow, Orange and Perfect Red.

Template 38T

-27-

The Spray *(See Illustration 39).*
Rose Hips *(See Illustration 40).*

11. Roll a large pea sized Red flowerpaste into a ball and then into an oval. Make different sizes. Hook a 26 gauge wire, glue the end and insert into the wider end of the oval shape. Press in at the base where you have inserted the wire. Leave to dry on your flowerstand. When dry, take a tiny ball of Brown flowerpaste, flatten and glue onto the pointed end of the rose hip. When dry paint with Confectioner's glaze. Tape down with Green florist's tape. Make 11 Rose Hips.

Ivy Leaves *(See Illustration 41).*

12. Roll out Yellow flowerpaste on a grooved board and cut out seven Ivy shapes with Ivy cutter IV2. Insert 26 gauge wire. Soften the edges with a balling tool and vein. Leave to dry.

13. When dry dust with Lemon Glo in the centre and Majestic Gold. Lightly dust the edges with Perfect Red.

14. Glaze by twirling the leaf in the steam of a kettle. This will allow the colours to blend and give a light shine. When dry tape with Beige florist's tape.

Maple Leaves *(See Illustration 42).*

15. Roll out Yellow flowerpaste on a grooved board and cut out three Maple leaves JM2. Insert a 26 gauge wire. Soften the edges with a balling tool.

16. Mark the veins with the pointed end of the veining tool (OP2) and leave to dry.

17. Dust the three Maple leaves with a variety of colours, Lemon Glo, Orange, Rose Leaf, Majestic Gold, Red Copper, Gold Green and Perfect Red. Steam. Repeat steps 15 and 16 with the smaller cutter JM3 and cut out six. Dust the six Maple leaves with a mixture of Majestic Gold, Red Copper with Chocolate Brown on the edges. Steam. When dry tape all the Maple leaves down with half width Brown florist's tape.

18. Tape the spray together with full width Brown florist's tape.

19. Dust the drapes using a mixture of Lemon Glo, Orange, Perfect Red and Majestic Gold. Roll out Yellow flowerpaste and cut out six flat Maple leaves JM3. Soften, vein and dust as before.

20. Attach the six flat Maple leaves to the top of the drapes using a piping bag.

TIP: A square piece of sponge on the handle of your paint brush prevents the bristles from touching the board accidentally.

39

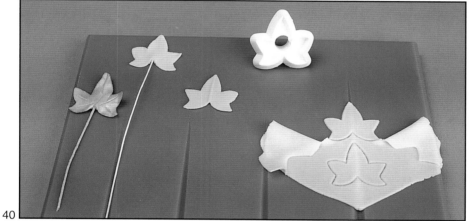

40

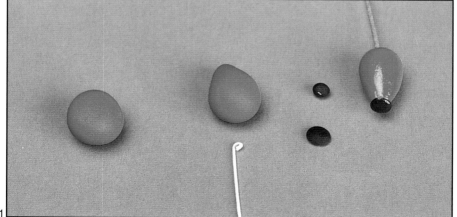

41

-29-

42

How to make the Flight of Fantasy Wedding Cake
(See Illustration 43).

(This cake first appeared in Cake Craft Magazine. The photograph is reproduced by courtesy of Ghost Images - Bob Challinor).

1. Coat the cakes and board with Ivory coloured Pettinice sugarpaste. Roll the 'Varipin' around the cake drum to give a material effect. Dust with Bridal Satin to give it a satin look. Leave to firm.

Border.

2. Tape 9 lots of 3 stamens onto 33 gauge wires using Lime Green florist's tape. Paint the tips of the stamens with a mixture of Violet and Orchid Mauve to match the paper ribbon. Paint with a little alcohol. Leave to dry.

Lace Flower Leaves.

3. Glue a tiny ball of paste onto a 33 gauge White wire. Leave to firm. (See Illustration 44).

Roll out White flowerpaste and cut out five Lace Flower shapes LF4. Work on one shape and cover the others with plastic. Cut round each shape to form a leaf.

4. Turn the flower leaf over and glue the top of the wire onto the back. Press well in.

5. Dust the tip of the leaf with Violet/Orchid Mauve and over dust with Cerise Sparkle. Dust the remainder Lemon Glo and over dust with Golden Glo Sparkle. Curve to shape and leave to dry.

6. When dry steam the leaves to seal the colours and bring out the sparkle. Tape with Lime Green. Repeat for the remaining leaves.

7. You will require 23 flower leaves for the border.

Top Cake. This trails from the middle cake to the top. You require 3 sets of stamens and nine flower leaves.

Middle Cake. This trails from the base cake to the middle. You require 2 sets of stamens and 5 flower leaves.

Base Cake and Board. 4 sets of stamens and 9 flower leaves. Facing the cake there are 3 sets of stamens and 5 leaves to the left joined by 1 set of stamens and to the right 4 leaves trailing just over the edge of the board.

43

44

45

Flower *(See Illustration 45)*.

8. Tape 1 long stamen and 6 short stamens onto a 24 gauge wire. Paint the ends with a mixture of Violet/ Orchid Mauve. Leave to dry. You will require 9 flowers.

Centre.

9. Roll out White flowerpaste and cut out primroses one F4 and one F3M.
10. Dust the edges with Yellow Glo and over dust with Golden Glo Sparkle. Soften the edges with a balling tool and cup in the middle. Glue the centre of the larger flower and place the smaller in the centre, alternating the petals.
11. Remove to the flowerstand. Glue the base of the stamens and carefully thread through the centre of the flower. Leave to set.
12. Roll out Violet/Orchid Mauve flowerpaste and cut out 2 sets of flowers using LF4. Remove the inserts with the pointed end of the veining tool.
13. Glue half way from the base of the flower and thread through the stamens making sure you have a 'lace calyx' over the heart of a primrose petal.
14. Glue the second set of Lace Flowers in the same way and interleave. Place in the flowerstand and prop the petals with 'Cloud Drift'. Leave to set. When set, dust the edges with Cerise Sparkle and the white centre with Bridal Satin. Steam to set the dust and bring out the shimmer.

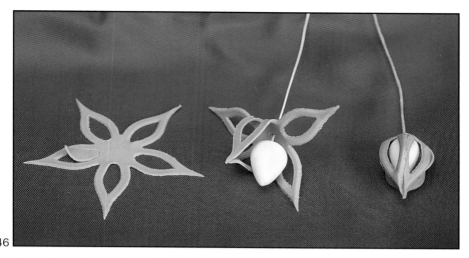

46

Bud *(See Illustration 46).*
15. Hook a 24 gauge wire. Make a cone from flowerpaste. Glue the hook and insert into the widest end of the cone. Dust the cone with Yellow Glo. Leave to set.
16. Roll out Violet/Orchid Mauve flowerpaste and cut out a set of flowers using LF4. Remove the inserts with the pointed end of the veining tool. Glue the ends of two opposite points and pinch together. Continue with the other 3. Over dust with Cerise Sparkle. Leave to set. Steam.
17. Roll out White flowerpaste and cut out several Lace Leaves using LL4. Remove the inserts.
18. Colour the tips Violet/Orchid Mauve and over brush with Cerise Sparkle. Dust the remainder Rose Leaf Green and over brush with Gold Green Sparkle. Steam. Tape each leaf with Lime Green tape.

Top Decoration.
19. Tape 1 Lace Flower for the centre and 3 Lace Flower Leaves around the Lace Flower.
20. Tape 4 Lace Leaves. One at the top of the posy and three at the base.
21. Tape 3 sets of stamens. Bend and cut the wire to allow the posy to stand.

Top Cake: 1 Flower, 4 Lace Leaves, 3 sets of stamens, 3 Lace Flower Leaves.

Middle Cake: 3 Flowers, 4 Lace Flower Leaves, 1 Bud, 3 sets of stamens, 3 Lace Leaves plus trail.

Base Cake: 5 Flowers, 4 Buds, 5 Lace Flower Leaves, 5 Lace Leaves, 5 sets of stamens. Plus the trail on the board.

TIP: Buy the ribbon first before you colour your paste,

47

How to make Chinese Lanterns *(See Illustration 47).*
Centre.

1. Hook the end of a 33 gauge White wire and 'glue' a pea sized Orange ball of flowerpaste onto the end.

2. Make some smaller Green balls of flowerpaste and 'glue' onto 33 gauge Green wires. Leave all to dry overnight.

Lantern *(See Illustration 48).*

3. Roll out Orange flowerpaste and cut out one Calyx cutter R11D for the lantern. Remove to the Orchard Pad (PD1) and soften the edges with the balling tool, but leave the tips.

4. Vein sepals on a leaf mould or leaf using the front of the leaf or mould so the veins are raised.

5. Mark 5 veins from between the sepals to the centre.

6. Thread and 'glue' a small ball of Green paste onto the wire from Step 1 under the dried centre.

7. Thread the wire through the centre of the Calyx (Lantern) and 'glue'. Arrange the sepals over the soft Green paste with the pointed end of the veining tool.

8. 'Glue' the tips of the Lantern and press some together and leave some open.

48

49

9. Repeat Steps 3 to 8 with Step 2 using Green and Yellow paste and Calyx cutter R11C for the smaller Lanterns.

10. Paint the stem of the Orange Lantern Orange. Glaze so the colour does not come off.

11. Dust the Lanterns with a Lustre Dust of choice.

12. Tape Lanterns onto a 24 gauge wire using Green tape.

13. The Devon Ladye Austrian and Brussels Lace cutters are used as a border. (See Illustration 49).

50

How to make the Rose of Sharon *(See Illustration 50).*
Hypericum Calycium or Aaron's Beard
Centre.
1. Roll out a long cone of Yellow flowerpaste and elongate the top until it is of equal length to the main part of the cone. Burn the end of a hooked 26 gauge wire and push into the base of the cone. Cut the top lengthways into 5 sections with a pair of scissors. Squeeze the base and fan out the top. (See Illustration 52).
2. Tape about 50 Bright Yellow stamens around the centre cone. Alternatively, use cotton for the stamens. Take about 50 cotton stamens, dip into gum arabic glue and then into Bright Yellow colour, liquid or dust. Leave to dry. Tape as above. Use the Petal Veining Tool (OP2) to spread them all out. Dust the centre tips Orange or Red.
3. Roll out Bright Yellow flowerpaste and cut out one F6 Five-petal flower. (See Illustration 52). Cut a little nick on the lefthand side of each petal with the point of the large Calyx cutter R11E and remove. Trim off the resulting corners and vein the petals with the Petal Veining Tool (OP2). Soften the edges with the balling tool (OP1) on the Orchard Pad. Place on a soft sponge and press in the centre to cup.

51

52

53

54

55

4. Make a little paste glue with Yellow flowerpaste i.e. mix with a little egg white until it becomes 'gooey'. Put into the centre of the flower. Thread the centre through the middle of the flower and place on the flowerstand (S1). (See Illustration 53). Prop in the desired position with 'Cloud Drift'. Leave to dry.

Calyx.

5. Roll out Light Green flowerpaste and cut out one F9 Five-petal flower. Place on the Orchard Pad and soften the edges. Put a little glue on the base of the flower, thread the calyx on to the wire and press gently into position underneath the flower.

Buds *(See Illustration 54).*

6. Roll out a ball of Yellow flowerpaste and push the hooked and glued end of a 26 gauge wire into it. Leave to dry. Roll out Yellow flowerpaste and cut out 1 F7 Five-petal flower. Soften the edges with the balling tool (OP1) on the Orchard Pad. Apply a little glue to the centre of the flower. thread up the wire and wrap round the ball. Fold over the petals to form something like a flat parcel. Squeeze the tips of the petals in as you fold them over. Repeat Step 5 for the calyx with F8 Five-petal flower. When dry, dust the edges an Orangey/Red.

Small Buds *(See Illustration 55).*

7. Roll out a cone of Yellow flowerpaste and push the glued end of a 26 gauge wire into the base. Mark vertical curves on the cone with a knife to represent dormant petals. Repeat Step 5 for the calyx with F9 Five-petal flower.

Template T50

Leaves.

8. The leaves are a darker Green. Roll out a tapered sausage, flatten (leaving a thicker piece in the centre) and cut out, using the template T50. Soften the edges with the balling tool. Mark the veins with the pointed end of the Petal Veining Tool (OP2). Glue a 28 gauge wire and, holding the leaf between your finger and thumb, insert the wire. When assembling, tape the leaves in pairs opposite each other and at right angles to the ones above.

How to make the Christmas Cake with Poinsettia and Holly Spray
(See Illustration 56).
Holly.
These can be made in any colour. I have made mine in White using Bridal
Satin, so I have used White wire. Make all the wire shapes for the cake
before you start dipping.

1. Shape the wire round a suitable cutter. Twist at base. Different sizes
look good on a branch. Make 4 small, 8 medium, 8 large.

2. Hold the base of the Holly between your fingers and bend the wire down
so it can be dipped horizontally into the liquid. Should it fail to adhere to
the wire simply re-dip.

3. Leave to dry in a block of dry oasis.

4. When dry, paint in the Green veins with dust colour and alcohol.

Holly Berries.
Small Red balls of flowerpaste glued to a 30 gauge Green wire. When dry,
paint with Confectioner's glaze.

To Assemble.
5. Tape 1 small holly shape to the top of a 26 gauge wire. A little further
down add the medium holly and some berries. Tape a medium holly to the
other side.

6. Next add the 2 large holly leaves alternating, and some berries, making
a small branch of 5. Repeat this three more times.

57

How to make the Poinsettia *(See Illustrations 57 & 58)*.
Stamens.
I bought 'ball' stamens and painted them Yellow, Green and Red with powder colour and alcohol. Fold about 13 stamens in half. Tape onto a Green 26 gauge wire. Cut the base of the stamens at an angle, then tape down the wire.

Flower.
1. Put Red colour on sponge, place the wire in the centre. Squeeze the sponge either side and pull through the wire. Set aside to dry thoroughly.
2. Fold over the top of the Red wire to give an elongated shape, twist the wire firmly at the base. Pinch the top. To make some of the petals different, set a curve to give movement. Make the petals from ½" to 1½" long.
You will require 6 small petals, 8 medium and 12 large petals. This is for the size of the Poinsettia shown on top of the cake.
3. Colour the Gelatine Red.
4. Holding the base of the petal bend the wire down so that the petal can be dipped horizontally into the liquid. Should it not adhere to the wire simply re-dip. Leave to dry in dry oasis.
5. When dry, paint in the veins using a fine paintbrush and Green powder mixed with alcohol.

To Assemble the Poinsettia.
6. Tape 6 small petals around the stamens at the same height.
7. Tape 8 medium petals in between the small petals.
8. Tape 12 large petals around the base of the medium petals. Arrange to form a circle.

To Assemble the Spray:
Tape each branch of Holly Leaves equally around the Poinsettia.

59

60

Side Design for Poinsettia Cake *(See Illustration 59 & 60)*.

The following is for one side of a square cake

1. Roll out White sugarpaste and cut out two N1 Six-petal cutter shapes. Make a centre vein using the pointed end of the Petal Veining Tool (OP2). Press a circle in the middle with the wider end of the veining tool. Dust all over with Bridal Satin. Dust the edges of the petals Red.

2. Roll a small ball of sugarpaste for the centre and press into a piece of tulle making an impression of tiny balls. Dust all over with Bridal Satin and the edges Red. Glue the back and place in the centre of the flower.

3. Measure and mark the centre of the side of the cake. Glue the back of the flower and press onto the side of the cake. Roll out White sugarpaste and cut out 6 Holly shapes using Holly cutter H4. Vein with Oak Leaf veiner (OL7). Dust the edges Red.

Board.

For each corner, roll out White sugarpaste and cut out 2 Holly shapes using H2. Vein with Oak Leaf veiner (OL6). Dust the leaves with Bridal Satin and the edges Red. 3 Red berries complete the corner design.

61

How to make Gelatine Honesty *(See Illustration 61)*.

1. Use 30 gauge White wire.

2. Colour the wire Beige by putting the colour on a sponge, place the wire in the centre. Squeeze the sponge either side and pull through the wire. Set aside to dry thoroughly.

3. Wind wire around a small rolling pin and tightly twist at the base. Shape the top of the Honesty by pinching the top with pliers to create a tiny point. (See Template 61T).

4. Dip into the gelatine using a mixture of Orchard White and White Sparkle to colour it. Dip one shape at a time. Remove the surplus on the side of the cup. Hold for a couple of seconds and place in dry oasis to dry. Should it fail to adhere to the wire simply re-dip. The drying period will take at least an hour. The gelatine film should feel like paper.

5. To make damaged Honesty make a few holes with a hat pin. Paint the holes and the marks Dark Brown.

6. To assemble the Honesty take a 24 gauge wire and Beige florist's tape and tape alternately down the wire

How to make the Primulas *(See Page 13)*.

62

63

64

65

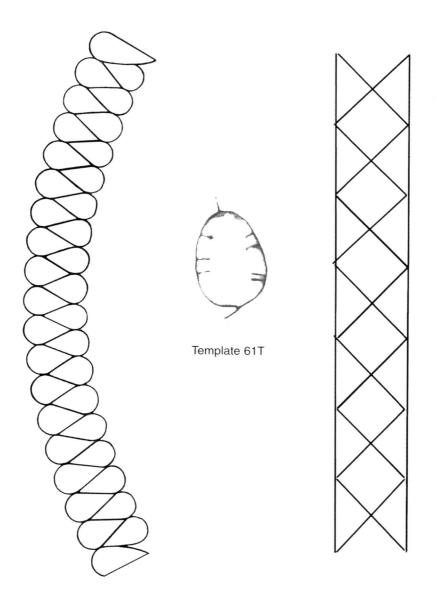

Template 61T

Template 26T

Template 27T

How to make Gelatine

1. 4 teaspoons (20ml) of hot water in a cup.
2. At this stage add the colour paste or powder.
3. Sprinkle 2 level teaspoons of Gelatine over the water and stir. Place the cup in a saucepan of hot water and keep hot. Do not boil. Stir until the Gelatine has fully dissolved.
4. Take care you do not create bubbles - if so leave to stand. You can also heat the Gelatine in a Fondue Set. This is very convenient as you have a night light underneath and the Gelatine stays at the right temperature for 'dipping',

Paste Glue   1oz sugarpaste of the same colour as the items
                    to be glued.
                    2 dessert spoons of warm water

Gradually combine together and place in the microwave oven for 1 - 1½ mins until the mixture boils. When cool, use as required. Store at room temperature, or refrigerate if not to be used for a length of time. If the glue is to be used immediately, then it is not necessary to boil it.

Tylose Glue   Tylopur CI000P
                    Water

Mix together in quantities representing 1 part Tylopur and 30 parts water. A convenient amount is made using an empty film container. About half fill with hot water, add approximately ⅛ teaspoon Tylopur, close, shake well and allow to stand for an hour. Shake again to mix well before using. A small squeeze of lemon juice added to the water enhances the keeping qualities!

Flowerpaste A (or Lace Paste).

250g (½lb) Bakel's 'Pettinice' or Craigmillar's 'Pastello'
only.

1 teaspoon (5mls) Gum Tragacanth

Rub 'Trex' on your hands and knead ingredients together until elastic. Wrap tightly in plastic cling film and store in an airtight container. Leave for 24 hours. Store in a cool place. This paste keeps well if worked through, say, once a week. Always keep tightly wrapped.

Flowerpaste D

450g (1lb) sieved icing sugar
5mls Gum Tragacanth **and** 20mls CMC (Carboxymethyl cellulose) - Tylose
10mls White Fat (Trex or Spry, not lard)
10mls Powdered Gelatine soaked in 25mls of cold water
10mls Liquid Glucose
45mls Egg White
(5mls = 1 teaspoon)

Sieve all the icing sugar into a **greased*** (Trex) mixing bowl. Add the gums to the sugar. Warm the mixture in a microwave oven 3 x 50 secs on a medium setting, stirring in between. Sprinkle the Gelatine over the water in a cup and allow to 'sponge'. Put the cup in hot, not boiling, water until clear. Add the white fat and liquid glucose. Heat the dough hook beater, add the dissolved ingredients and the egg white to the warmed sugar, and beat on the **lowest** speed until all the ingredients are combined. Turn the machine to maximum speed and mix until the mixture becomes white and stringy. Grease your hands and remove the paste from the machine. Pull and stretch the paste several times. Knead together and then cut into 4 sections. Knead each section again, and put into a plastic bag, then in an airtight container and keep in the refrigerator. Let it mature for 24 hours. This paste dries quickly so, when ready to use, cut off only a small piece and re-seal the remainder. Work it well with your fingers. It should 'click' between your fingers when ready to use. If it should be a little too hard and crumbly, add a little egg white and fat. The fat slows down the drying process and the egg white makes it more pliable. Keep coloured paste in a separate container. This paste keeps for several months

*This eases the strain on the machine considerably.

All the tools referred to in the text can be obtained
from good sugarcraft retailers or by post from:-

Orchard Products

51 Hallyburton Road
Hove, East Sussex, BN3 7GP
ENGLAND

Tel: 44 (0)1273 419418
Fax: 44 (0)1273 412512

**The Lace Cutters (pages 2, 12 & 35) can also be obtained from
Devon Ladye, The Studio, Coldharbour, Uffculme, Devon EX15 3EE,
England. Tel: 44 (0)1884 841316**

There are other books in this Sugarcraft series, by PAT ASHBY

Flowers and other ideas - Book 1
ISBN 1 872573 01 0
More Flowers and other ideas - Book 2
ISBN 1 872573 02 9
Ideas with the Garrett Frill and other Cutters - Book 3
ISBN 1 872573 03 7
Creative Ideas for Cake Decorators - Book 4
ISBN 1 872573 04 5
Great Ideas for Cake Decorators - Book 5 + Index
ISBN 1 872573 05 3
Blossoms to Bonsai - Book 6
ISBN 1 872573 06 1
Flowers and Favours - Book 7
ISBN 1 872573 07 X
The New Orchard Lace Collection - Book 8
ISBN 1 872573 08 8
Sugar Art Deco and more Floral Inspirations - Book 9
ISBN 1 872573 09 6
The Varicut Cutter and other marvels - Book 10 + Index
ISBN 1 872573 10 X
The Lace Flowers and other brilliant ideas - Book 11
ISBN 1 872573 31 2
The Lace Leaf Cutters and other Floral Gems - Book 12
ISBN 1 872573 32 0
The Flower Swan, Textured Ideas and Flowers - Book 13
ISBN 1 872573 33 9
Incredible Edible and other ideas - Book 14
ISBN 1 872573 34 7

Photography by G.Ashby

Printed by RARE Repro, Hailsham, East Sussex